How Ghosts Travel

James J. Siegel

Spuyten Duyvil
New York City

©2016 James J. Siegel
ISBN 978-1-941550-74-8
cover photo by Judy Wilson
author photo by Desi Tafoya

Library of Congress Cataloging-in-Publication Data

Siegel, James J.
[Poems. Selections]
How ghosts travel / James J. Siegel.
pages cm
ISBN 978-1-941550-74-8
I. Title.
PS3619.I377A6 2016
811'.6--dc23
2015032086

*To every friend, loved one, teacher, and mentor
that supported me in this strange thing called poetry.*

And to all the ghosts that roam the state of Ohio.

Prologue

1   How Ghosts Travel

Part I

5   Mayfly
8   County Fair
10   Blizzard Of '78
12   Fishing Photo, Circa 1984
13   Sisters Of Mercy
15   Tornado Season
17   Easter Sunday
19   Industry
21   Death Star
24   Boy Scout Blue
26   Map
28   Michigan Firecracker
30   Massillon
33   Dorm Room
35   Summit Street
37   Lake Erie Dead Zones

Part II

41   Ghosts Of Ohio
43   Mary Bach's Fingers
45   Rented Home
47   Traditional Ache
48   Ithaca
50   Dark At 2 PM
51   Jason
53   Ouija
54   Roseville
57   Serpent Mound
59   Flatlands

61	Little Pills
62	Dawn Of The Dead
64	Ohio Border Commute

Part III

69	Identifying With Licking County
70	Remains
72	The Road
74	Numbered Stones
76	Search Dogs
79	Murder Of Crows
81	Quarters
83	Reliable Transportation
85	Skyline
87	Saturday Afternoon Horror Movies
89	Orchard
90	The Other Side
92	Chippewa Lake
95	Acknowledgments

How Ghosts Travel

I've seen ghosts
move like liquid —
like rain creeping through
a crack in a window.
This is how they enter
and rearrange the furniture,
turn the faucets on,
peel the sheets from the bed.

They understand the engine
of running water
and ride the currents,
the channels and connections
that tie Ohio together.

It's a slippery secret
that Lake Huron shares with Erie.
And Erie can't resist,
runs its mouth to the Maumee,
the Sandusky and Cuyahoga —
a thousand souls sliding down the state.

Look at the St. Mary's River
rushing out of Mercer County
only to return again
with a handful of souvenirs —
stowaway souls
on their way to Fort Wayne.

This is how the dead travel —
attaching their energy
to the rising tides of Indian Lake,
shifting their weight
until they reach the Shelby Reservoir.

They dissolve into foam
on the surface of Raccoon Creek,
charged particles
bending the tides,
rippling into the Great Ohio.
They touch the shore of Kentucky,
take a human shape
and walk again.

It explains the inexplicable,
how boys that drown in the Little Miami
can chase the pretty girls
playing in the suburbs of Cincinnati,
how a man shot on the docks of Cleveland
can roam the empty homes of Lexington.

Part I

Mayfly

Life is short
for adult mayflies.
They mate
over warm lakes,
shallow riverbeds,
until it's time
for the females to drop their eggs
on the water's surface.

Exhausted from age
she rests on a wave —
slides into the mouth of a trout.

Meanwhile, the men
fly off by the millions
to live out their last days.
A biblical plague
descending on the sides of buildings.
A living tapestry
of spindle bodies
baking on hot concrete,
on every humming telephone poll,
every picnic table at the Frosty Freeze.

They were silent little house guests,
Jehovah's Witnesses
that wouldn't go away.
Lounging on front porch swings,
twitching their antennas
on the screen doors,
they waved to the mailman,
to the neighbors next door.

A gory horror show
on my early morning paper route
when they popped like overripe grapes
under the wheels of my bike,
exploded under the weight
of a heavy weekend edition.

A good scare
on summer evenings
when they caught you off guard,
floating like phantoms
from the corners of the garage,
the darkness of the rose bushes,
to brush the sides of your face,
rest in the tangles of your hair.

They were everywhere —
a congregation of wings
in the parking lot
of St. John the Baptist,
clinging to the stained glass,
the bells in the steeple.
Sometimes they wandered in
to tap their toes on the organ keys,
walk the length of St. Joseph
from his sandaled feet
to the baby Jesus
cradled in one arm.

But mostly they loved
the rusted anchors of the marina,
the boat propellers slick with slime,
the beer-soaked coolers
stacked on the rocking docks of the river.

Mostly,
they were like my father,
looking for peace
after long, hard weeks
of bending metal into car parts.
No Sunday services —
just a tackle box,
a brown-bagged lunch
and the afternoon light
shining off a fishing lure.

His hymn simple —
If I want to find God,
He'll be on the lake.

Sometimes I see Him
when the insects die,
return again
to haunt the places they left behind,
when my father comes home
sun-burnt and beaming
with a fresh catch —
pails of big-mouth bass,
their bellies full with mayflies.

County Fair

Those red tents have been resurrected
off state route 25. They fill the sky like rust-colored clouds,
like a summer storm sliding off the lake.

It's a sure sign the town will die
for a day or two at least
or until the fairground closes its gates.

It has never been my thing —
the blue-ribbon pigs,
the kids with their cotton-candy hands
screaming on the tilt-o-whirl.

I would rather go downtown
where it looks like the Rapture has come.

All God's faithful rising
and falling on carousel horses
as sinners wander the streets.

Shuffling shoes down the avenue
every ordinary sound seems sacred —
the leaves dragging their dead bodies down the block,
the flag at the post office flapping its stripes.

The wind carries a jukebox tune
from one of the corner bars
and I swear I can hear the record stop,
flip,
and begin to play again.

It should seem that the world has slipped away
with the banks and bakeries left behind,
the drugstore windows filled with dust,
but it's never seemed more within reach.

And at night from my bed
while the fireflies cluster like galaxies,
the earth will echo back
the fireworks display,
the grinding of gears from the tractor pull,
and I will drift away.

Blizzard of '78

When I was born I brought along
the blizzard of '78.

Weeks past my due date as though
the winter waited with a warning,

waited patiently to tell me —
The world is going to harm you.

I banged and kicked at the front door,
the barometer dropped,

the sky's seams ripped apart,
catching the Midwest off its guard.

A state of emergency
from Detroit to the Kentucky line —

salt trucks idled in the ice
as the county closed the turnpike,

the National Guard was called
to pull bodies from buried cars.

The Ohio Valley went dark
when I saw my first threads of light.

Power lines and telephone wires
snapped like rubber bands,

choking the life from furnaces,
freezing the old inside their homes.

My screams filled a hospital hall
while some people escaped the cold —

an elderly man found face down
in a field off Route 547.

I was told I wailed for hours
and the winds yelled back in reply,

the winds surveyed the damage
satisfied with the aftermath —

roofs collapsed under the weight of snow,
cats and dogs missing in the drifts.

Others found dead with shovel in hand —
a heart attack in the front yard.

Eventually I found a calm,
my cries lulled me to slumber,

the January night silent,
as though the argument was made —

twenty-eight inches in three days,
fifty-one dead across the state,

and I was wrapped in warm blankets,
taken home to start this life.

Fishing Photo, Circa 1984

I was once a little boy in high waters,
toe-head, bowl cut, clutching
his first big catch. We have the photo to prove it.
We may even have the rod that almost snapped
when the line struggled to find the surface.
        I'm glad you have that memory —
your flannelled arms around my life-jacketed body,
net at the ready,
ready to wrestle in that walleye or sheephead,
that sea-monster sized big deal. It was a big deal to you.
Father and son.
But I used to wonder what I had done
to deserve the 6 a.m. on Sunday,
crying my way out of bed,
begging to stay at home. You always said no.
I dreaded the sway of the dock,
the warming of the boat engine, the stench
of burning fuel, fishy water. And the drifting.
All day long, anchored yet rising and falling.
Dad, it still makes me sick,
        to think where your mind drifted
        when I refused to bait my own hook.
        Perhaps you drifted to other disappointments —
        the outfield where I sat on the grass,
        thumbing together daisy chains
        or the long summer days when real boys
        traded baseball cards for trouble
        while I dressed dolls with the girls down the street.
The Lake Erie waters were like your eyes,
gray and hard to navigate
when the wind picked up.
But even a boy in high waters could tell
you got the boy you never wanted. Except
for the day we pulled something out of the deep waves,
something so great we had to take a picture.

Sisters of Mercy

I would always take the dare,
tiptoe up the convent stairs
(closed since 1969),
knock on the door,
then run away and hide,
waiting for something to answer.
God, how I prayed for silence
as panic found its place
at the base of my spine,
then climbed
like a little nun ascending a tower,
to ring a bell in my head.

Once, I found the courage
to creep inside,
Mother of God
chipped and busted on the mantle,
the mirror in the foyer shattered,
the dining room desecrated
with inverted stars,
six, six, six,
the spray-painted pranks
of kids bolder than I.
My flesh cold
I pressed my ear to the wall,
listening for the rattle of a rosary,
for the notes of a hymn
still clinging to the organ
like a decade of dust.
But nothing —
only my sigh of relief

and my footfalls on the floorboards
as I ran to find my friends,
to say *I did it*,
I went inside, survived
with no sign of the Sisters,
dead or alive.

Today, the convent is still there,
crumbling and wrapped in thick ivy.
I feel a chill
when I walk by,
but the fear is different now
Not a fear of seeing,
but of never seeing —
a mist in the form of a woman,
her habit tight about her face,
or a black mass sliding past the window
darker than a winter evening —
something that says there is more
than plaster peeling,
or the remains of holy cards
wrapped in the wallpaper
and left to wither
until the walls give way.

Tornado Season

He shakes cyclones from a crayon —
raw umber and burnt sienna
spiraling in the distance
of a construction paper landscape.

Clouds are colored crimson
like carnations crushed and unfolding
the way they must have looked on Palm Sunday, 1965,
when mass was cancelled
and the trailer park disappeared.

So his churches are closed
and his houses are dark
when his first funnel touches down
in a supermarket parking lot.

With one tight gripped scribble
cars are flung in loopty-loops,
landing on their hoods like stunned little bugs,
tires spinning towards the sky.

He knows this story from the seasons
huddled in the basement
with a transistor radio, flashlights
and a box of crayons
while the maples do backbends
and the perennials shiver.

He doesn't know how the air
tasted like tin, copper pennies on the tongue
and lemonade stands left behind
by children called in from the street.

But he's seen the newspaper clippings,
the fierce forces on microfiche,
the photos of the Point Place Yacht Club,
its boats stacked like minnows in a net.

And he knows about the families
pulled from their living room windows.
        There they are on the corner of the page —
stick people squiggles,
arms out and waving
saying hello to heaven
or good-bye to earth.

Easter Sunday

I feel anything but new
with these chickadees,
with these pastel dresses
covering the girls' knees.

I've never been inspired
by the resurrection,
the empty tomb,
Doubting Thomas
poking fingers in the wounds.

For me it is the unchanged,
the slow end,
the long drawn death
that drives a nail
through the hands of the Midwest.

It is snowstorms in March —
the winters that wheeze
one last icy breath,
sputters and coughs
a light dusting of flakes
on the buds of daffodils.

It's the gold foil
peeled from the flesh
of a chocolate bunny
while Valentine's candy
melts on a kitchen shelf,
coconut and jelly cream
congealed in a heart-shaped box.

The bees buzz from their hives,
fat and lazy
from weeks of pollinating roses,
daisies bursting from sun and rain,
while the neighbors refuse
to tear down their Christmas lights —
wires sagging from porch railings,
limp as lifeless body parts,
green and red bulbs
burning in the heat of spring.

And it's the dead leaves of autumn
fossilized under banks of ice,
the church parking lot
a pool of melt and run off
reflecting the skies of April,
the bells in the steeple
clanging and screaming
Christ has risen,
Christ will come again.

Industry

I miss wandering through the wastelands with you,
the waist-high grass moving as we moved
into places we didn't belong —
the construction sites, the abandoned houses,
the automotive graveyard where we sat in the shell of a dead Chevy
and compared family histories.

Our fathers both factory workers
on strike every six months
and down at the union hall
for donations of canned foods,
government assistance.
That would not be us.
There were other worlds
tucked away inside our world.

Running around in your brother's hand-me-downs you held me,
helped me over barbed-wire fences
that separated the manufacturing plants from the paths
winding deep into the woods. So deep it's safe
to dump the things we do not need.

There was a strange beauty in the box springs
left to wither in the weeds and ferns. The dirty old drainpipe
where someone's sneakers sailed along in the runoff.
Beer cans, paper bags left behind
by other latchkey kids. And that Zenith radio
smashed against the rocks. "Made in the USA"
branded on the side. Guts and gears
spilling out. Wires waving like ghostly fingers.

Those hiding places are now harder to find,
but today the air tastes like burned-out machinery,
powdered milk and all the shit that lingers
in blue-collar skies. You should see the way it still slithers
from the stacks like thin white ribbons uncoiling,
evaporating into the clouds.

Death Star

I want to go back to that time,
somewhere around age five

when I had Luke Skywalker in one hand,
Chewbacca in the other,

when my grandmother's white shag rug
was the frozen planet of Hoth,

my Rebel figures saddled on their tauntauns,
my AT-ATs towering in the distance.

And when Princess Leia was taken prisoner
(because she was always taken prisoner)

Stormtroopers would escort her
to the bookcase by the front porch,

each shelf of Ellery Queen mysteries
just another floor of my Death Star.

Grandma sipped coffee in the kitchen,
smoothed the creases from her newspaper

while the Price is Right was cut short
for breaking news I didn't understand —

something about the Soviet Union,
the threat of nuclear weapons,

and satellites in the heavens
to shoot missiles from the sky.

The sun would lay its lazy rays
over the endless expanse of the davenport,

reach for the mid-century TV tube
to throw a glare on President Reagan.

But I didn't care,
I had my own battles to fight —

an Emperor with an evil agenda,
an Empire with a deadly weapon.

My father walked a picket line,
while my mother searched for work

and still I didn't care
when the long days were mine,

when I took my Ewoks outside
to pretend the flowerbeds were Endor.

The other day I found Wicket
hanging out in a desk drawer,

shoulder to shoulder with Greedo,
that villainous scum.

My Millennium Falcon
is boxed up in the attic,

and Jabba the Hutt lost his arms
the year before junior high.

I want to find them,
glue them back on his green slug body,

blow the dust off the bounty hunters,
Boba Fett and all the rest,

pose them with their plastic guns,
with Han Solo in carbonite.

It's sad — grown men playing with toys,
but then again so is the world

with its bunker bombs,
its soldiers kicking down doors in Afghanistan.

My father retired from blue-collar work,
my grandmother dead and gone,

her home now my sisters,
her shag rug sold at an estate sale.

The dark side is never really defeated,
so what the hell —

I'll let the Jawas chase the droids
on the desert of my hardwood floor,

let Yoda raise my X-Wing
from a moldy corner of the basement,

and I'll dig up Darth Vader,
to rebuild my Death Star.

Boy Scout Blue

Like any Midwest boy
I knew this color —
deeper than the sky over Camp Lakota.

It borders on black and loves
a good ghost story in the shadows
of the Tar Hallow Forest.

You should see it bob for apples
at the Halloween jamboree —
its jester's grin biting red flesh.

It's the great future hope —
you want that shade of blue
when the wind kidnaps the map.

It knows the rocky trails of Ohio,
where to find running streams,
the path of the stars.

It finds the plants we cannot eat,
the insects that we can —
knows that carpenter ants taste like lemons.

But every pigment changes shades
depending on the position of the sun,
the needle drag on the compass.

Young hikers take a tumble
and something different bleeds
from scraped knees and dirty palms.

It's the indigo bruise —
more painful, more destructive
than a father's disappointment.

So lonely it begs
for the solace of merit badges,
the honey-gold embrace of a neckerchief.

So lonely it burns
field mice with lighters,
spiders with matches.

It has a knot for every occasion —
the timber hitch for dragging logs,
the handcuff knot for securing wrists.

The weakest are always tied to trees,
the frost of the wilderness floor
presses violet kisses to the lips.

The same kisses form on the lungs
of older boys treading
the inkwell waters of Lake Madison.

They flail their arms and scream
but skies still blacken
and no one comes.

Unforgiveable, monstrous —
it is a jet engine darkness taking shape
in a cabin window when the moon disappears.

Map

I unfold it
careful near the creases
where time has left them tattered
like tectonic plates
ready to tear landmass from landmass.

This is the culmination of a life
spread flat on the table
where miles are reduced to inches.
I drag my index finger over a piece of land
the city council will one day annex for a town park
and they'll pull the tarp off a statue
dedicated to a general in the War of 1812.

I can't tell you the exact timeframe of this topography;
years after my grandfather fought the Germans,
years before my father feared the prospects of Vietnam.

My grandmother, her children,
lived their whole lives here
somehow content with what they had.

It is a lesson I am trying to learn,
to appreciate this scale,
the acres of triangle-tipped trees
scattered among the subdivisions,
rows and rows of square little homes
on streets named after civic leaders,
regional fauna.

The railroad tracks bend like a stray strand of hair,
sliding past the hospital where I was born,
along the graveyard where my relatives rest.

There is peace with everything in reach.
Each neighborhood a thumbnail
or two away from the schoolyard,
the schools an eyelash from the factories
fuming on the riverbanks.
Even God and country close at hand —
the VFW hall just two blocks from the Methodist Church.

But still my eyes drift
to a faded-blue splotch of lake
flowing off the page,
to roads that touch the wrinkled edges of the city limits
and suddenly stop.

Michigan Firecracker

Bottle rockets and jumping jacks —
roman candles and parachutes —
all illegal in the state of Ohio.

So you bought them over the border
in towns like Erie and Monroe
at firework super stores
that sprouted each summer
like backyard dandelions.

It was a pilgrimage for you —
a covert operation
in the evening of July 3rd,
in the morning of July 4th
for something to burn
brighter than the fizz of sparklers
showering flames of rain
from a child's hand.

I never understood the need for something more,
unsatisfied with charcoal snakes,
bored with the pop and puff of smoke bombs.

You needed to hold powerful names
like Dragon Tears and Phantom Wheels.
You needed rooftops bathed in the light
of Machine Gun Shells,
Molotov Cocktails.

There was danger
from police patrolling the parks,
on the lookout for Military Satellites,
troublemaker kids launching
Outer Space Jets.

There was risk
in the last minute release —
the M-80 lingering too long,
the discharge of fingers from hands,
the blast of skin from bone.

And then there were the nights,
sleepless in the summer heat.
The whining flight of firecrackers,
the bedroom walls bursting
with the glow of passing comets.

Those Independence Days were lost on me —
lost in the perpetual percussion,
the haze of falling stars.
Then I saw your eyes —
wide and alive
when your spark struck the fuse.

A grounded thing
heaved its earthbound body,
looked east, looked west
as though deciding
a destination to lay claim —
The heavens of the Great Lakes,
the borders of Canada,
the mountains of the moon.

Any place was possible
when the lift charge ignited
and the darkness was subdued —
for a second or two —
by a phosphorescent fury,
the gold and silver filaments
blazing trails to the polls,
neighboring counties,
distant hemispheres.

Massillon

If you are boy
born in Massillon, Ohio,
you will be visited
by the booster club.
They will come bearing gifts —
a little rubber football
placed in your basinet —
Go Tigers!
emblazoned on the side.

It's a simple gesture,
a gentle push that says
God damn it,
you will learn to throw.

You will be baptized
in driveways and backyards
during that winter-waiting period
before the pre-season,
when boys learn the fine art
of the wrist snap,
when their frozen breath
is thicker than the smoke
spilling from the mills.

There will be penance
for the things your father did,
for the things he couldn't do —
the incomplete pass,
the sideline sack.
You will need to do it better
than generations before.
Charge the defensive line
with 100 years of history
stacked on your padded shoulders.

You will eat of this,
drink of this and pray for this
in the locker room,
in the huddle,
in the months before the big rivalry.
Our Father, who art in heaven
let us beat the bulldogs,
let us kill McKinley.
And you will taste this
when those scoreboard seconds
tick off another victory,
another head bowed,
another knee touching the field.

And if all goes as planned
you will fall in love with this,
commit yourself to the autumn clatter —
young bodies colliding,
the formations on the field,
the coaches whistle.
You will fall in love with Friday nights
when the stadium lights burn
brighter than Venus and Jupiter.
You may settle down
with a scholarship at State
or settle in for your life
bending steel at the plant

But if the opposite is true —
if you go long for that Hail Mary pass
and it fumbles from your fingers,
letting down an entire town —
remember, you can cut back
past bleachers,
past parking lots
with their crepe paper floats,

past Republic Steel,
the Family Farm and Feed.
Rush to the Lincoln Highway,
that famous road
that charges through Massillon
to other territories,
to other states
on its way to another coast.
Keep going and thank the Lord
you learned how to run
as soon as you learned to walk.

Dorm Room

He whispers about the girlfriend he left back home,
how he might rush in the fall
or find a part time job in town.
His words are soft from the top bunk,
a change from his daylight varsity voice.

I can't tell him I won't be sleeping
only dreaming
of how long this thing has been after me.
It feels older than the mattress
passed down over the decades
from one confused freshman to another.
Perhaps there was a 1950s version of me
slowly peeling back the layers
gently like warm blankets.
And underneath the pure, Christian heart
was something that didn't add up.
Maybe his head fell
on algebra books, penciled equations,
classroom scribbles summing up
hours of daydreams,
daydreams that knew
there was no going back
to a bed in a room
in a home that died so long ago.
It died with the baseball cards,
the model planes and all the rest
of the crafty cover-ups.
I am sure there was a family name
on high school transcripts, generations
that were waiting for graduation
to be born. But there was a secret
in sock drawers, a revelation
in the undertone of late night talks
with a boy from southern Ohio.

He says he might change his major,
that he is in no hurry to marry,
but he thinks he'll make a good father.
I try to let my body rest
on all the hard years beneath me.

Summit Street

It is late
and the streetlights purr
like stray cats. Raccoons rummage
through trashcans.

I should wait until tomorrow to explore
but there are words to rehearse in my head.
And it's better to see that old street
while sensible people are in bed.
Better to sneak up on it
like a hibernating bear.

Nothing has changed
except the bank has a fancy new sign
illuminated with the temperature and time.

And everything is smaller —
train set miniatures of a town.
Memory rushes back like an engine through a tunnel.

Suddenly I am three feet tall
with the sight of the schoolyard,
its faded four-square grids.
The library, the Lutheran church,
every place I learned to be quiet
looks somewhat sunken and sullen.

Even the corner drugstore
looks sad and slumped over
like it just heard bad news.
That is where we bought quarter candy,
where I was bucked off the handlebars of some boy's bike
because I said something silly like
I think I like you.

I ran the whole way home
holding my hands over my mouth,
blood breaking through my fingers.

There are hours of darkness
to lose myself in
but my parents are waiting up for me.
It has been months since I've seen them.
There is so much I need to tell them.

Lake Erie Dead Zones

The fishermen go farther
and farther each year,
past West Sister Island,
as far east as Sandusky Bay
searching for walleye,
for the steelhead trout
that left the smoke-stacked shores,
the shipyards and refineries,
the high levels of mercury and lead.

Even my father says,
they don't bite like they used to.

And still they come —
their tackle boxes bursting
with fat night crawlers,
minnows from a bait shop
that won't last another summer,
its burned out Bud Light sign
a relic of some other time.

They cast lines on a lake
where the chemicals have killed the oxygen,
constructed tunnels of dead space
where the fish can't breathe.
Picture them —
wide-eyed and confused
when the gills fail,
the fins frantic with fear.

Nature knows what to do,
knows when to move on.
People are different.

They sail
past the Edgewater Café
mummified in vines,
its tables left for termites.
Watch them drift down streets
where grocery stores closed,
or never opened,
past the town's first school
rusting like an old nail.

Even jobs disappear.
Freight trains find new routes.
factories close their door,
and they still cast their nets
hoping to find something in the water.
They fill their lungs with fumes,
take deep breaths
and float along.

Part II

Ghosts of Ohio

When I was young
these stories would come
and sit on the edge of my bed,
like a mother looking after her child,
a mother unaware that she is dead.

The five cemeteries of Athens
form a pentagram
when connected on the map.
And in the center is the university
where the walls in Wilson Hall bleed,
where a girl in room 428 still screams
years after she died.

Then there is the torso killer
of Kingsbury Run, collecting limbs,
leaving them in baskets and burlap bags
along the Cleveland riverbanks.
And when the sun goes down
headless shadows surface
behind Hart Manufacturing,
under the Cuyahoga bridges.

Even in that hospital on the hill,
with its dark tuberculosis ward,
condemned now, and silent on summer nights,
something moves on the top floor,
a fluid shape in the window waves
like curtains or a patient's gown.

These things do not scare me anymore.

Not like waking to a new day
unchanged
from the day before,
the ground thick with ice
and apparitions at the window
formed from last night's frost.

Mary Bach's Fingers

> *For the Wood County Historical Museum*
> *(Bowling Green, OH), the keepers of Mary's fingers.*

If you're looking for your fingers
we have them at the museum.

Index, middle, ring fingers
in a jar of dried formaldehyde.

You see, we like our souvenirs,
our mementos of history,

and you were part of history —
the county's bloodiest murder.

Maybe you don't know what happened,
don't even know that you are dead.

Just drifting and wondering why
half of your hand has disappeared.

I don't like having to tell you
your husband was responsible —

took all his anger out on you
when the crops failed and the farm died —

hacked you apart with a corn knife,
left you like a slaughtered heifer.

I'm sure you know how men can be,
enraged at first then guilt-ridden,

throw a punch then apologize,
do the crime then run to confess.

It's never fair but you should know
they hung him by the courthouse stairs

while families paid to see the show
and picnicked on the town square lawn.

The truth is locked in a glass case
where your fingers are on display

along with the Bible Carl read,
the rope that choked the life from him.

He is probably down in hell
or some dark place where sinners go.

But you are in a strange grey space,
in a world that bumps against ours.

Your energy touches our plane
and we can hear whispers through the walls.

If that is you it needs to stop.
You're scaring the museum staff.

Visitors scream and don't come back
when they hear crying in the hall.

You must quit moving furniture,
titling frames on the second floor.

We will take care of your fingers,
you don't need them anymore.

Rented Home

The house settles
for another hundred years
and my body shutters
with the shame that this is it. Another night
side by side, back to back,
a mutual silence
while the walls sigh.

This is all we ever wanted —
an old relic on the block with affordable rent,
something we could handle with your wages and tips,
with my college degree gone to waste.
Three bedrooms, two baths, a hallway
that shifts when I blink
and think of the past.

In lucid dreams
or walking slumber I leave you. I find my way
down basement stairs
to that place containing old days,
where the wall becomes a door
beyond the washer and dryer,
behind the hot water tank.

We have debated what that room could be —
the reason why it hides from the eye.
It is the home's coal storage before the gas furnace
or the first owner's secret workroom
where he could spill sawdust in silence.
Or perhaps it was some bootleggers business
when prohibition dried up the Midwest.
Or maybe it was a stop on a journey,
a waiting room until night,
for the Northern Star.

It does not matter to me. That room
of crumbling brick is far below
the bending floorboards, below the kitchen
with its quaint cupboards, fine china stacked
in neat, undisturbed rows. It is below
the family room filled with furniture
we found at flea markets, garage sales —
our first purchases together.

In that bed we bought for a bargain
you sleep. And I go to that space to create timelines,
searching for the one that takes us
in different directions.

Traditional Ache

He is gone
and I wait for it
like Christmas day,
like cycles of the moon. I wait
for it with silver bullets,
with my best friend on speed dial
and still nothing. That fur-covered
folklore crawling out from under the skin,
that heartache turned to hunger —
I know it. Three times before
it has come. Punctual and petty,
it is clockwork
like winter wandering back again,
digging its claws into the rooftops. And I know
this all sounds dramatic
like some lunar event,
but in other years, under a different sky,
I stared into the yellow eyes of that mythology,
that old tale of two people,
their inevitable tragedy. It is the torture
of teeth, the cut of canines. But tonight
there is nothing but the silence
of the suburbs, the neighborhood dogs
disturbing the dark with cries and barks,
begging to find what prowls in backyards,
hides behind barns or in the shadows of tool sheds.
It is only some small beast
come to claim some old bones. Tonight
it is only the distant howls to heaven
chasing off a predator that flees
on four legs
or two.

Ithaca

So you escaped
to that land of hills and hipsters.

It is not much different from Ohio,
except for the snow in September,

and the art galleries in the Commons,
the college dropouts begging for change

or the remains of your cigarette
before you toss it to the cold, night air.

Then there are the roads that rise
like they are reaching for the winter sky.

Nothing like here
where the land is flat and predictable.

Let me get this out of the way:
Living your life is letting me down.

So you paint every day,
inspired by the icy mounds of Ithaca,

the foamy white waters that crash
and spill into the Fall Creek Gorge.

You've captured it on every canvas
and soon they will beg for your work —

the coffee shops filled with kids from Cornell,
those art exhibitions on the campus lawns.

This can't last forever,
but it could last a mighty long time.

Your brushstrokes may learn to adapt
from icicles to bright blades of grass.

You may leave behind your landscapes,
trade them for portraits in the parks,

for the students with their poems, their guitars,
relishing the rare days of summer.

So I wish all the best for you,
but not really.

Dark At 2 pm

December rain dances with swaying swings
in the playground. It drums its feet
on dirty trails where human remains were found.
I wonder if the dead feel the cold
during mid-afternoons in winter
when children sit at decaying desks
watching clouds collect thunder and darkness.
There are lessons on arithmetic, the Revolutionary War,
but the world is filling up with loss
like storm drains after a torrential night.
Something feels heavier than science books
with their explanations for everything. Distractions
take the young away from bus stops
and homework on Monday evenings.

Even I have been taken away
from my writing, from a warm cup of tea
to see the darkness at 2 PM, the sky swirling
and obscuring the tops of church steeples.
There are poems to finish and words
I have yet to get down, but I am drawn
to the grounds in the graveyard,
soft from the day's weather, its fresh burials.
I wonder if the long gone shiver
when we are gently pulled away from living.

Jason

When I was around seven or eight
I would stay up late and watch
the Friday the 13th movie marathon.

Not many people know this,
but Jason wasn't the killer in part 1.
It was his bat-shit crazy mother
butchering camp counselors with creative flair,
sometimes a bow and arrow,
sometimes a clean knife thrust
through the bottom of a cot.
(I can still see the blade tip
bursting from Kevin Bacon's chest.)

And not many people know
the summer before second grade
I stayed away from the basement
only tiptoeing down to grab a toy
then racing back up
taking the stairs two at a time.
More than once I thought I'd die —
my father's ice fishing boots behind the furnace,
his flannel shirts hanging on the line,
were enough to trick my eyes,
force a panicked wail
loud enough to wake the neighbors,
enough to make me wet my pants.

    Eventually, Jason and I drifted apart.
He went to Manhattan, even outer space,
and I went to college in Bowling Green, Ohio,
where the farmland looked like Camp Crystal Lake
and my dorm mates were perfect Hollywood doubles
for beer binges and midnight skinny dips.
But death came without the help of a hockey mask.

      Between winter and spring semesters
students disappeared from campus.
Coming home from Christmas break,
their vehicles slipped on ice,
flipped over the interstate guardrails.
They vanished when sickness came,
when chemo and meds interfered
with biology and chemistry class.

Even the actors in those Friday slasher flicks
were meeting mortality off the screen.
Harold, mutilated with a meat cleaver in part 3,
was crushed in his car on a California highway.
And Mark, the wheelchair-bound heartthrob
who took a machete to the face,
lived on to fight AIDS
until AIDS won.
Then there was Brenda.
After her corpse was thrown through a cabin window
she left Hollywood for a husband,
five children and pancreatic cancer.

      It's cancer of the pancreas
that will take you the fastest.
You start to decline before you know why.
I've seen its handy work in a hospice bed
and watched the way flesh turns yellow
when the liver capitulates. Still
it makes you wait.
And it makes you wonder
how you could ever be afraid
of a movie marathon
when you were seven or eight.

Ouija

Ask whatever you want,
But remember — the dead
Can lie like the living.

Don't say I didn't warn you when
Everyone has opened that door.
Fingers on the planchette, sliding
Gently from letter to letter, from "yes" to "no."

How old were you when you died?
Is it cold on the other side?
Just tell us who you are.

Know that you will get answers that sound
Like a shy child or a young southern belle,
Meek and humble that you would care.
Notice how they say "please" and "thank you,"
Or how they confide in you that they wish to be alive.

Place the board on the shelf and it will tumble back.
Quiet hours all alone, they will beg to talk.
Rattle a window pane, the chair beneath you.

So you go back to keep them company, but
This time the messages are bolder, rude perhaps.
Upsetting little phrases like *I hate that you are alive* or
Victory would be living in your body. And they will reveal
What you thought was a little girl was an old crone from
Xenia, Ohio, or a teenage boy that once dissected rats in
Youngstown. Worse still something alive that has never lived —
Zepars, dukes of hell, underworld royalty, unable to say goodbye.

Roseville

The broken locks on the chain links
will tempt you to venture inside,
and the sun will bathe the towers
with November's lavender light
as though some spark of life abides
behind the Roseville Prison walls.
But do not mistake for human
the dark shape that wanders those halls.

No souls damned to roam forever
the death of the warden's office —
his red rotary telephone
heavy with ancient dial tones,
ghost calls to the governor.
No murdered guards left to patrol
the catwalk's eternal night watch.
Only rows and rows of cellblocks,
the rusted bones of mattresses,
broken porcelain and crumbling stone.

No innocent men still waiting
for an overturned conviction
or the sad lingering voices
pleading for prayers from the living.
Every prisoner has been paroled,
transferred to some purgatory,
to some other-side waiting room.
Nothing remains to be released.

Just something in solitary —
a black shape that never lived
but burst forth into existence
after decades of midnight screams,
the yearly bed sheet suicides,
shower room strangulations,
brains beaten with iron bars.

No calamity was too small.
It took them all and multiplied —
knuckles broken under batons,
the low muffled cries of inmates,
blood that stained the infirmary.
Every misery collected
into an oil spill of pain
until it learned to take a form,
learned to float and move on its own.

Time alone leaves it to hunger
and so it searches corridors,
sends the rats and rodents to flee.
It hunts for the familiar taste —
nitroglycerin and sawdust —
the delicacy of cordite,
the last breath escaping a corpse.
That fattened mass of agony
will carry these things forever.

And one day it will come to you,
undulating in the mess hall,
billowing like smoke in the morgue.
It will pass you by, pass through you,
and you will feel a sick disease —
the deep sharpening of the shank,
the shiver of the death row walk.

You will feel centuries of confinement
like two deep thumbs behind the eyes.
A lifetime of someone's decline
radiates out like a signal,
a message hidden in airwaves.
It answers your urgent question —

these horrors live on forever
while the autumn sun unshackles,
frees itself from the western skies,
and the vault of the stars unlocks.

Serpent Mound

You are my Serpent Mound,
my mystery coiling and uncoiling
below the beating heart of Ohio.

An effigy etched in earth —
thirteen hundred feet long, three feet high,
visible from the Midwest sky.

No one knows why it was built
or how we should have met
and found a common purpose.

It may have been astrological —
the way that structure matches
the architecture of the stars,

mirrors the constellations above,
just as we were born
under the same rising sign.

It could have been the seasons —
the unfurled tongue tasting
the summer solstice sun,

the tail touching the equinox.
Winter withers, spring awakens
and still you are here.

Some argue it is geography,
location making it possible
for two people to find each other,

to build beauty over tragedy —
a monument constructed
where a meteor made its impact.

It is the great collision of lives,
the one in a billion chance
we celebrate with symbol, ritual.

A monolithic charm
keeping watch over old Brush Creek,
guaranteeing safe passage

by waterway or to the other side.
It is the theory of direction
that I believe in.

The land so vast
it is easy to get lost,
confuse east from west.

So the body is a compass,
a man-made landmark
with unmovable roots.

Miles unravel,
gravity changes its mind
and there it is —

the great shape of you,
the great magnet
that pulls us back to the birthplace,

the sacred ground
where we found one another
and wrapped our lives together.

Flatlands

The dawn could not break through
the confederate, gray gloom,
fog, like cannon fire,
looming over the flatlands.
My boots broke the stubborn ground,
cracked and frozen in the October chill.

Some things will always be,
like the wind that comes in
riding on cavalry horses,
lifting the back of my jacket,
stampeding down Main Street,
ruffling the rebel flags in townie bars.

The war never came this far north,
but the locals think differently.
This field is filled with stories of soldiers,
tired and dirty from marching,
horses huddled and guns slung
as letters are written home.

I only see the car parts factory
where a farmhouse once stood,
the Pentecostal church with its revivals
louder than battle cries,
the rolling expanse of horizon
we could have made our home.

There was a life for us
in the bonfires that bloomed each spring,
with the ones we loved tending the flames,
with the open spaces that could be reined in.
But all this was left for the rows of corn
bowing their heads to the cold ground.

From my college town to the county line
these things are reenactments,
scanning the distance for a ghostly glow,
for proof that things are more than memories.
Now it is only the autumn morning
making shadows into Union dead.

Little Pills

I line up all these little pills
like long rows of corn.

They take me back to other drugs,
to other fields. Skipping class,

parking the car at the end of a county
road. Wandering past the stalks

until the highway went away,
until it was safe to pass the pipe,

to inhale the possibilities. In those days
it was only pot, mushrooms once. And

it never took long for me
to rise above the priorities

of exam week, graduation day,
writing the perfect resume.

       But it was more than this.
It was life at the end of the season,

a body like December dust,
dancing over the dead acres,

floating high above the dormitories,
the frozen hands of the clock tower.

These days I look down to see
the yellow kernels that allow me

to manage an eight-hour work day,
to pull the car out of the driveway.

Dawn of the Dead

The dim morning light
once again flickers grey and white
like an old film purring on the projector.

I am sure I will see a clumsy corpse
creeping down the street
pulling one bum leg behind him.

I've seen these days before —
and where there is one
there is certain to be more.

It makes me want to board the windows,
pull a heavy dresser in front of the door,
run for the basement stairs.

      But that would be foolish.
The basement is darkness and dead ends,
curtain calls for B-movie stars.

Instead, there is safety in the attic,
an oversized trunk on the trap,
a window to the roof.

With a transistor radio,
secret missions to the kitchen,
there is no need to ever leave.

And tucked deep in the shadows
are memories in mausoleums
begging to come out and play.

They are not to be feared.
They are paperbacks sleeping in dust,
old 45s in rusted cookie tins, shoeboxes

of letters that seemed worth saving,
and the negative proofs of photographs
that turned up missing. I will wait

for the day's thin dawn to shine
through each celluloid strip,
each frame of familiar days.

It will pass the time wondering
when the army tanks will roll up,
when the sky will bleed Technicolor.

Ohio Border Commute

I.
The rays of the day are resting
in the cracks of my windshield
as the sun struggles to blossom over the strip mall.
Everything is in bloom –
the smoke that buds from the tip of my cigarette,
the wildflowers waving from the side of the road.
Each day they grow taller
alongside a modest white cross,
a symbol of some tragedy
wrapped in glass and guardrails.

II.
Every day the radio
plays the same song. A repetition
of traffic backs up to the Ohio border,
bumpers nudging bumpers.
Everyone is in a hurry
for places they don't want to be.
Nothing moves except the sparrows
flying in formations. They rise up
like heat from the highway,
like the exhaust of semi-trucks. They rise from sacred ground
marked by two pieces of lumber and flee
as though remembering
some important place to be.

III.
The evening comes in early now
with clouds sullen and somber
like the eve of a suicide. That white cross
looks like someone's Halloween prank
with the trees naked and skeletal. Today
a silver balloon was tied to the axis,
where the compass points meet. It bobs along
with each passing car, each commuter
eager for home, the television set,
their spouses and children.

IV.
Another holiday jingle
drifts up from the car speakers.
Everything is a burial of white.
A makeshift memorial pokes out of a snow bank.
A big, fat Santa grins from the top of the mall,
knee deep in Michigan's first snowfall.
He grips a banner framed in garland:
seven more shopping days.
Someone will never make it to Christmas dinner,
their best friend's New Year's party.

Part III

Identifying with Licking County

County of a hundred ghost towns
and counting.   I understand
the woman walking there.

Her headstone sinks behind the hills
and still she paces rotted floors,
moves through walls
where once there were doors.
And she'll keep walking
after the foundations fall
and the roof crumbles
because her memory has
nowhere else to go.

You cannot stop
what kept repeating.   It is why
the Buckeye Scenic Railroad is nothing
but dead grass in the shape of tracks
and yet the train whistle
scatters starlings on the sky.

We cannot expect the past
to just stop speaking
or the Hanover firehouse to forget
the horses' heavy hooves
that knocked the stable walls. Listen
for one last muffled nicker
trapped for decades in the air.

There will always be enough loss
to fill the silent spaces left behind.
It's the only explanation
for the shadow sliding past the banister,
the porch door banging shut,
the lighter hissing sparks,
and your brand of cigarette
slipping through the screened windows.

Remains

The suburbs started sneaking in the summer
you taught me how to smoke a cigarette,
how to crush it on the bottom of my boot,
flick it into the cornfields. Yours always soared
like arrowheads, while mine tumbled like tomahawks.

It was the summer you taught me about girls
with guitars and your tape deck killed The Pretenders —
chewed them up before Chrissie Hynde could say,
those were the happiest days of my life.
It was your idea to tear the guts from the cassette,

one filmy knot spiderwebbed around your fingers.
It was my idea to let it loose, let the wind take it
like an offering to the land. June through August
we did nothing but drive through town
while cement mixers churned. We did nothing

but watch the distance ripen with the dust and dirt
from digging. Layers of sweat stuck to my skin
like secrets I was too afraid to tell —
there was no one else I wanted
to spend my days with. Monday through Friday

drinking Natural Light, tossing the cans
from the car window, listening as they sputtered
under the wheels, laughing as we sang
and the speakers cracked and popped, *Now*
we're back in the fight, we're back on the train.

We laughed and we listened to backhoes
break ground for a gas station, the highway expansion —
until it all just stopped. Bones of an ancient civilization
unearthed where a parking lot was supposed to be.
One man, one woman — buried with what they kept sacred:

Pieces of pots, effigy pipes, primitive tools. So
we watched when the tribal leader came
to burn sage, tobacco, chant the native tongue,
wrap the remains in burial cloth. A moment of silence —
then the engines turned over one more time.

That was the summer they finished the industrial park,
and I promised I'd die in Ohio
with our bits of cigarettes, our greatest hits,
waiting to be found deep in the earth,
waiting to be placed under museum glass.

The Road

It is a deep wound
in the flesh of a field — a scar
that runs the length of two townships.
Take me back there
and tell me that story
of bloody handprints
burned on bus windows.

Tell me how that Yellow Bird
still barrels along,
how the road rumbles
when the moment remembers
the wreckage and the lives
that let go.

In those teenage tales
the dead are said to walk
the miles of dirt and gravel,
dart through the dense woods
like hunted deer.

    How I wanted that —
to hear the crunch of stones
near the passenger door,
watch the darkness shift
into a human form.

    I know you wanted it too,
to believe the whining of the wind
was the squealing of loose wheels,
voices trapped in a tin can.

And the ghostly orbs
bouncing in the distance
were another disappointment
as they fizzled from the fog at midnight
to reveal headlights on a passing pickup.

Imagine what we could find
if we returned,
let the engine die
and waited for the past
to cross over from the other side.

    Take me back
and we can watch the moon
conspire with the trees
to make shadows
in the shape of children
running down the road.

Numbered Stones

It is too easy to forget
names and dates and places
where we left the dead.
That is why the pauper's field
is overgrown with crabgrass,
with bougainvillea
knuckle-tight around the rusted gates.

I don't think they are coming this year —
those boys doing community service,
bussed in from the juvenile halls,
the learning disabled classes.

I will miss their silhouettes
shifting behind iron bars,
their thin bodies
heavy in the haze of a summer morning.

I will miss wondering what they did
to deserve drifting in a sea of swaying grass,
counting down the day in numbered stones
from one to one hundred and on
until the weeds have been cleared away.

And I will miss creating back stories,
fictionalizing the crimes they committed —
luring stray cats to the dark corner of a garage,
snapping their soft necks
just to hear the sound.

Or the pop of the air pistol
on the Catholic schoolyard,
the twirl of plaid skirts
as the girls lift their hems
to inspect the pink bruises
blossoming on their skin.

I would wonder if they wondered
about the bones below their feet
and if they spent the hours pondering
unclaimed human remains,
old women and orphaned children
coughing blood until their last breath.

Perhaps it was all just penance,
just work to be done,
and they don't remember
the drone of lawnmowers,
the swatting of flies from the eyes,
or the way the stones lean away
like listening in on a secret
when the land dips south.

Search Dogs

The search dogs are sleeping —
their muzzles cradled
on weather-worn paws,
filthy from the forest floor,
sore from the miles
circling the reservoir
and back again.
If you let them
they would chase the day into its cave,
they would brave the darkness
if lantern light could break
the thick, shadowy night.

I am just as stubborn
when I have picked up the scent
of something familiar,
when I'm trying to put my finger
on locations I have lost.

Like that farmer's field —
barren and abandoned
as though it were a gift willed to me.
My own private parcel
where I sat alone
and smoked alone,
inhaled the rising sun,
exhaled violet sunset skies.

It has to be where I left it,
where Sugar Ridge meets Highway 92,
where the landscape was nothing
but mounds of earth —
rows and rows of dirt
where stalks grew tall
before turning to a testament
of the things that quit.

It was always west of town
where that clapboard barn
struggled to stand on its own —
nothing left inside
but the ghost cries of Holsteins,
the old ropes and rusted tools
that once pulled
sweat and blood from the body.
It was here I kicked the dust,
watched it rise like a memory.
It was here I promised
I would never be so empty.

If I could find it I could feel
what it was to be there again
in a time before things changed,
before the world rearranged,
ran away and went missing.

Maybe it's the seasons
that throw me off the trail,
the days that go shortchanged
a little more each month.
Perhaps it's the gravel turned to asphalt,
the roads changed to new names.
Maybe it's nature —
clouds that spiraled down,
destroyed trees, dismantled buildings.

This chase continues
long after I submit to slumber,
long after evening has come
with black gloves to strangle the light.
Fragments of that field,
pieces of places I've forgotten
spool out as dreams go deeper —

I run rocky paths behind the water tower,
explore dried riverbeds at the county line,
pick up clues where the railroad trestles rot.

I go on hunting
like the dogs in the mud room,
in the warm glow of the stove.
Even they know time is not on our side.
Watch their eyelids
flutter like insect wings.
Watch their scruffy hind legs
jerk and fidget
as they pull on a phantom leash,
begging for more slack
as though trying to say,
We are getting closer,
this is the way.

Murder of Crows

It is late winter
  and the sky is filled with them
drifting on the air.

Wings spread and gliding
  over lonely county roads,
dark as a blood clot.

Soon they will descend
  like bitter old memories
in search of their roost.

And like memory
  there is always a season
for them to come home.

Floating down like ash
  they'll cover the chimney tops,
the tips of branches.

They'll hang together
  huddled like young high school boys
hiding cigarettes.

In their marble eyes
  I will see recollections
of old flight patterns.

I am done with them,
  with their matching uniforms,
with past migrations.

But they are stubborn,
        cursing among each other,
refusing to leave.

When they are ready
        they'll unfurl like a black flag
let loose on the wind.

Quarters

Anything silver would do —
nickels or dimes —
but quarters were the greatest find.

Whatever we could dig
from our car's ashtray,
whatever we could excavate
from the caverns of our couch cushions
added up to something great —
a pack of cigarettes
shared on the university steps
while the quad echoed a sadness
for the students that had left,
back to their hometowns
waiting tables, saving tips
for another semester.

We should have done the same —
picked up extra shifts
to pad out our paltry paychecks.
We should have collected our coins
in jelly jars or milk jugs,
saved them for laundry-day Sundays
at the Bowling Green Wash & Dry,
turning the pages of a paperback
while the dryers fumed and churned,
the cool summer air
sliding in from open windows.

We should have packed what we had
in tight bank rolls,
cashed them in to stock the cupboards —
instead we counted them out
on convenience store counters,
pushing pennies to the clerk

until we had the right number —
two cans of beer and Parliament Lights,
a handful of free matches
as we headed out the door.

We had library fines and student loans,
a grace period set to end.
It's all I thought about —
my twenty-something slow motion
winding down and stalling out,
the reality of the world ready
for change.

So we hid away at happy hours
with dollar shots and dollar drafts,
fed the juke box, the pool tables,
listened to the billiard balls
rumble from their slumber.
And we filled ashtrays, filled the air
with smoke from our lungs,
with the notes of our laughter.

I think of those months,
those years wasted,
content on going nowhere,
but safe somewhere in Northern Ohio,
the rent due, the utilities late,
dirty socks and shirts
erupting from their hamper.

I smile when I turn my pockets inside out
and another lifetime falls to the floor.
It's a crescendo —
a bell breaking,
the honest sound
that I never needed anything else.

Reliable Transportation

Let's take this Nissan Pulsar
and see how far we can go
in the graveyard of December,
in the dawning of the new year.

Let's test the tire treads
on the black ice of the turnpike,
test the signals on the dashboard —
see how long it takes the oil light
to glow a dangerous shade of red.

There is little I can offer.

The cassette deck is frozen
and the windshield wipers
waved their last good-bye.
But you already know
my transportation is unreliable.

You were the one
who rigged my muffler
with an unraveled coat hanger,
super-glued my side view mirror
when I hit the garage door.

You were the one
who could lift the hood,
fiddle with hoses and belts
until you worked a miracle.

And now a new miracle —
you've had enough of New York,
the frigid touch of the Finger Lakes,
the reckless winds of Rochester
that speed down the streets,
reach for the bones under your coat.

The winter is only worse
when we are all alone
and New York knows
a special kind of cold
that fights the first of spring.

Rest your feet on my glove box
and see how this engine still turns over,
how the headlights are bright enough
to break through the falling snow
that pounds the Pennsylvania roads.

There are cigarette burns
on the bucket seats
but buckle up
and we'll pass Pittsburgh by evening,
hit eastern Ohio soon after.
The seasons change earlier every year
and the temperature rises
as the odometer ticks off the miles.

Yes, the floors shake,
the windows rattle
when we accelerate,
and I may need a few bucks
to top off the tank,
but I can still get you
where you need to go.

Skyline

It scares me to death —
the Skyline Drive-in
lurking in the woods
of New Lexington
off State Route 13
like an old hermit
confused by a world
that left him behind.

So little remains.
Every car speaker
ripped out of the ground,
replaced with wild ferns,
patches of crab grass.
The old ticket booths
nowhere to be found.
And the access road
backed up with traffic
on Saturday nights
is now a dirt path,
a place for the trees
to sag their branches,
to lighten their loads.

But do not tell me
that Skyline is dead.
The concession stand
has somehow survived
despite the windows
broken and shattered,
the candy cases
covered in cobwebs.
Look at the menu
still fixed to the wall —
Pepsi a quarter,

cigarettes a buck.
Then look to the east
where the screen still towers,
begs for attention,
arms stretched to embrace
the vast vacancy,
weather worn and torn
from wind and rain and
years of forgetting.

It makes me shiver
when the moon projects
on that monster screen
a double feature
starring the shadows
of stray cats strutting,
night birds gliding by
to search the forest
for something to hunt,
something soft to kill.

If you don't believe
take a long deep breath
on a cloudless night
when the wind's just right
and you'll smell popcorn
buttered and burning,
and the fumes from cars
idling their engines.

Saturday Afternoon Horror Movies

Don't leave.
      The front yard is filled with death clinging to the elms,
screaming under foot. Besides, the sun won't be out today.
It will sleep inside its crypt until the autumn tires of its stay.

      We have the living dead on local access, masked psychos
with butcher knives on cable. We can slip some rum into our cider,
drill the eyes into a jack-o-lantern and keep a tally of the body count.

      So you noticed
the poltergeist in the kitchen throwing around dirty dishes,
and the bed that goes unmade for days.
I've just been too busy
tracking the noise like a pounding
in the walls or in my chest,
something that is here,
      but gone.

      Tell me if you hear it
over the chainsaws on the television. Tell me
if you feel that chill like a specter just sat down in the corner.
      All these disturbances come crossing over
when my mind wanders to the orbs in photographs,
our long ago debates on what teases the lights on and off at midnight,
what rattles the doorknobs one by one down the hallway.

      It must be so much more than the dead trapped
and lost in boarded up farmhouses, the slippered-feet of the old
shuffling for centuries in condemned nursing homes.
      Maybe it's the power of a moment or a time,
the power of a pain so great it left pieces to puncture our layers.

We used to know how to waste a Saturday. Your knee
touching mine under a heavy blanket, the ghost of cigarettes
still haunting the ashtrays, the wind like the beat of bat wings
on the side of the house.

There was a time when the fear of such things passing
and changing was unreal to us. Unreal like resurrected psychopaths
or the way a teenage girl can't run through the woods without tripping. Stay
and explain to me how that died.

It did not die violently like blood splattering on the screen.
It crawled down slowly to the living room floor
to taste the dust, to let the choke of October
settle in its throat.

Orchard

There are no more bees
crawling through the corridors
of rotting apples.

No more ember glow —
gold on gold from leaf and sun
as day slides away.

There is nothing left
but the acres of thin limbs
on winter's pale skin.

Free of all burdens,
the clutter of past seasons,
voices can be heard.

It is a language
the land seems to understand
when the branches sway.

Words tossed to the wind
seem to say, *the past is done
and we are okay*.

The Other Side

On the other side
we have no bodies
but we drink Pabst Blue Ribbon
in rickety lawn chairs
on your front lawn.

Don't ask me how it's possible —
it just is.

Like the sun
always in mid sunset
and the pack of cigarettes
on the table between us
never runs out.

Here we smoke all evening
because we have no lungs.
And we laugh
until our non-existent stomachs hurt,
laugh as loud as we want
because the neighbors don't complain —
they have no ears
and only hear what they want to hear
like choirs of crickets
heralding the night,
owls in the trees
ruffling their wings.

Eternal Indian summer
with just a whisper
of winter on the wind —
that is what we feel
on our translucent skin
to remind us when seasons changed,
to make us believe
time will come to an end.

There is nothing to see here
but the rabbits chasing
the last threads of the day,
the crows landing
just to squawk
and fly off
when the 4x4s
speed past your house
on their way to a town
that is no longer there.

It's beautiful —
the way the diesel fuel
burns and rises
to touch the Armageddon sky.

Beautiful
how it looks like Ohio
but feels like heaven.

Chippewa Lake

Everything will end
        like the Big Dipper coaster
at Chippewa Lake.

It is not easy
        to imagine the midway
sleeping through summer

or the Tom Sawyer
        steam engine beached on the shore
dead as an old carp.

But these things happen.
        Factories close, families move,
gears sigh one last time.

The Starlight Ballroom
        is now a pile of steel bones
from last year's arson.

And the Tumble Bug
        tucked away in Kiddie Land
has toppled over

from the weight of time,
        from teenagers sneaking in
to climb on her arms.

I know how this looks —
        these mechanical corpses
left for cruel deaths.

But the land will bring
        a kind and gentle passing
that comes with the spring.

The season creeps in
        with tight vines for the turnstiles,
the chain link fences.

It fills the empty
        spaces of the Ferris wheel
with thick birch branches,

coaxes the dogwoods
        to crane their necks through the slats
of the coaster's track.

All will surrender
        like the delicate remains
of a white-tailed deer

left to decompose
        with the wild violets that bloom
from the soft ribcage.

See how the lift hill
        of the Big Dipper rises
like a slender spine

reaching for the limbs
        of blue ash, for the embrace
of the day's last light.

ACKNOWLEDGMENTS

The following poems in this collection first appeared in the following journals and publications.
"Mayfly" The Good Men Project, July 2014
"Ghosts of Ohio" Paper Street
"Rented Home" Assaracus Issue 9
"Traditional Ache" Borderlands: Texas Poetry Review, No. 29
"County Fair" Assaracus Issue 9
"Fishing Photo, Circa 1984" Assaracus Issue 9
"Tornado Season" The Broken Plate, 2011
"Dark at 2 PM" The Toledo Review
"Skyline" Jenny, Issue 4, Spring 2012
"Little Pills" Assaracus Issue 9
"Murder of Crows" Blueline, Volume 29; Assaracus Issue 9
"Identifying With Licking County," Jenny, Issue 4, Spring 2012
"Reliable Transportation" Assaracus Issue 9
"Saturday Afternoon Horror Movies" The Fourth River, Issue 3; Assaracus Issue 9
"Chippewa Lake" The Cortland Review, Issue 51
"The Other Side," Jenny, Issue 4, Spring 2012
"Massillon," Codex Journal

JAMES J. SIEGEL is a San Francisco-based poet and literary arts organizer. He is originally from Toledo, Ohio, which has inspired and fueled much of his poetic work. He was a scholarship recipient to the Antioch Writers' Workshop in Yellow Springs, Ohio, and his poems have been featured in a number of journals including The Cortland Review, Borderlands: Texas Poetry Review, Assaracus, The Fourth River, and more. He was also featured in the anthology, *Divining Divas: 100 Gay Men On Their Muses.*

www.ingramcontent.com/pod-product-compliance
Lightning Source LLC
Chambersburg PA
CBHW020946090426
42736CB00010B/1284